GRANDMA
KETTLE'S
Pies & Cookies

GRANDMA KETTLE'S
Pies & Cookies

Phil Kettle and Leslie Kettle
with help from Grandma

(Stoddart)

A BOSTON MILLS PRESS BOOK

Canadian Cataloguing in Publication Data

Kettle, Phillip, 1931-
  Grandma Kettle's cookbook

ISBN 1-55046-070-6

1. Cookery.   I. Kettle, Leslie, 1967-
II. Title.

TX714.K48   641.5   C92-093914-7

First published in 1992 by
Stoddart Publishing Co. Ltd.
34 Lesmill Road
Toronto, Canada M3B 2T6
(416) 445-3333 Fax: (416) 445-5967

A BOSTON MILLS PRESS BOOK

The Boston Mills Press
132 Main Street
Erin, Ontario N0B 1T0
(519) 833-2407 Fax: (519) 833-2195

The publisher wishes to acknowledge the support of the Canada
Council, the Ontario Arts Council and the Ontario Publishing Centre
in the development of writing and publishing in Canada.

Contents

From left to right: Grandmother Kettle (age 18), Great-grandmother Gillespie and Aunt Bessie. Great-grandmother Gillespie allowed her daughters to watch her cook, but insisted that it was easier for her to do the cooking herself than have the girls mess up her kitchen.

Preface

Christine Cunningham Kettle (nee Gillespie), my mother, grandmother to my children, maintains that on the day she was married, she could not boil water without burning the pot. In her childhood home, her mother had done all the cooking — her daughters would learn soon enough. And so my mother did. The recipes which she developed, adapted and borrowed during fifty years of marriage have become family heirlooms and part of a tradition.

Cooking became a way of life for Christine Kettle, and an area in which she excelled. So much so that friends and groups continually request favours in the form of cakes or pies for bazaars, rummage sales and important social gatherings. Approaching her eighty-fifth birthday, Grandmother still uses a 10-kilogram bag of Five Roses flour each month. Since it is difficult for her to carry this weight, it has become our part of the deal to keep her supplied with baking supplies in the brands which work best for her.

In mid-February 1992, while out for lunch with a grandson, Grandmother fell off a restaurant bench and broke a hip. One pin, one plate and one week later, she was home; six weeks later, she was baking pound cake for something or other.

Many of these heirlooms were originally handwritten by Grandfather on paper now held together by layers of Scotch tape. The recipes for some of the items in this book were previously nonexistent or were misleading in their use of less-than-exact quantities. A pinch of salt or a handful of sugar required translation into common measurements.

It was granddaughter Leslie who pushed to have the recipes interpreted and recorded for future generations. Leslie spent a great deal of time mixing and cooking beside Grandmother to learn first-hand the art of creating good pastry and light-textured cakes. Her experience made the translation easier. It was only after the recipes had been compiled that the idea of a cookbook took shape.

In an age when we all claim to be calorie and cholesterol conscious, the advent of a cookbook containing cake and pastry recipes may seem ill-timed. But just place a plate of butter tarts beside a dish of celery sticks and see which gets eaten first.

Phillip G. Kettle
Burlington, Ontario
April 15, 1992

The Kettle-Gillespie clan regularly went on picnics to Port Dalhousie, near St. Catharines. Grandmother's cooking was always the highlight. This photo was taken in 1932. From left to right: Uncle Alex, Aunt Bessie, Uncle Jimmy, Aunt Doris, Grandmother Kettle, Grandfather Kettle. In front: Phillip Kettle

The same group fourteen years later.

Bikini Bars

²⁄₃ cup	sweetened condensed milk	150 mL
1 tsp	vanilla	5 mL
½ tsp	salt	2 mL
2½ cups	coconut (desiccated)	625 mL
2 cups	dates (chopped)	500 mL
¼ cup	maraschino cherries (chopped)	50 mL
½ cup	walnuts (chopped)	125 mL
2 squares	chocolate (unsweetened)	

- Mix the condensed milk, vanilla and salt together.
- Add the coconut, dates, walnuts and cherries to the mix.
- Spoon the dough into an 8"x8"x2" cake tin. The tin should be greased, lined with wax paper and greased again.
- Bake at 350° F/180° C for 30 minutes. Leave to cool.
- Remove from the pan when cool and peel off the paper.
- Ice with Butter Frosting (see page 46).
- Melt the squares of chocolate over hot water or in the microwave oven and drizzle over the cake.
- Cut into narrow bars to serve.

Recipe Hints

Dried fruits were used extensively for these recipes because when Grandmother learned to cook, fresh fruit was not always available and was expensive. Electric refrigerators were not found in most households, and dried fruits were more easily stored. Baking was done every week.

Date and Nut Drops

2	egg whites (beaten)	
½ cup	white sugar	125 mL
½ tsp	vanilla	2 mL
½ cup	walnuts (chopped)	125 mL
2 cups	Corn Flakes	500 mL
½ cup	dates (chopped)	125 mL

- Mix all ingredients.
- Drop spoonfuls onto a cookie tray.
- Bake at 325° F/165° C for 10-15 minutes.

Recipe Hints

The egg whites should be beaten stiff for best results.

During the Depression you wasted nothing. If the foodstuff was not acceptable as originally intended, another use was found or created for it.

Corn Flakes were one of the few dried breakfast cereals available. Quite often they were left unsealed and lost their crispness. The kids refused to eat them at that stage, so they were used in cookies. The 2 cups of flakes in the recipe are better if they are not fresh. These cookies were often made after a cooking session which left a quantity of egg whites to be used up.

Empire Biscuits

³⁄₄ cup	white sugar	175 mL
¹⁄₂ cup	butter	125 mL
2 cups	Five Roses flour	500 mL
¹⁄₂ tsp	baking soda	2 mL
1	egg	
	a few drops of lemon extract	

- Cream the butter and add sugar.
- Add the flour and baking soda until the dough mix is crumbly.
- Add the egg and beat lightly.
- Add the lemon extract.
- Knead the dough on a board. Roll the dough to ¹⁄₄" thick and cut it into shapes with cookie cutters. An ordinary drinking glass makes a useful cutter.
- Place on cookie sheets. Bake at 350° F/180° C for 10 minutes.

Recipe Hints

Before there were Mixmasters, cooks would beat the dough to the correct consistency. The modern grandmother uses a food processor or a Mixmaster. The dough for these cookies should be mixed until it becomes soft but does not stick to the bowl. Mix until the dough holds together.

This is a layered cookie. The top and bottom sections are put together with raspberry jam between them. A butter frosting is spread on the top, with a glazed cherry for decoration.

These biscuits are a creamy colour when cooked.

You may freeze the parts separately or put them together and freeze for future use.

Instead of a butter frosting, a shiny frosting can be used.

Icing

1 cup	icing sugar	250 mL
¹⁄₄ tsp	salt	1 mL
¹⁄₂ tsp	vanilla	2 mL
1¹⁄₂ tbsp	cream	20 mL

Hermits

½ cup	butter	125 mL
½ cup	brown sugar	125 mL
2	eggs	
2 tbsp	milk	30 mL
3 cups	flour	725 mL
1 tsp	baking soda	5 mL
1 tsp	cinnamon	5 mL
1 tsp	nutmeg	5 mL
½ cup	walnuts (chopped)	125 mL
1 cup	raisins	250 mL
1 cup	currants	250 mL

- Cream the sugar with the butter; add the eggs, then the milk. Mix the dry ingredients separately, then add them to the butter mix.
- Fold in raisins, nuts and currants last.
- Drop onto a cookie sheet.
- Bake at 350° F/180° C for 15-20 minutes.

Recipe Hints

Few households could afford to purchase cookies during the Depression. Each week cookie tins would be filled with homemade cookies for lunches and treats. Hermits are very good for lunches, providing a sweet treat with solid food value.

This recipe makes a lot of cookies. Grandmother varied the cookies' size according to their intended use: for children's snacks they were dropped onto the cookie sheet with a tablespoon; for company a teaspoon would be used.

Oven temperatures can vary considerably between stoves. Each cook will need to make a batch of cookies to check the time and temperature for best results.

Other nuts may be used instead of walnuts.

Oatmeal Cookies

1 cup	butter	250 mL
1 cup	brown sugar	250 mL
1	egg	
$\frac{1}{2}$ tsp	salt	2 mL
$\frac{1}{2}$ tsp	baking soda	2 mL
1 cup	Five Roses flour	250 mL
$\frac{1}{2}$ tbsp	sour milk	8 mL
$2\frac{1}{2}$ cups	oatmeal (or rolled oats)	625 mL

- Cream the butter and the brown sugar together.
- Add the egg.
- Add the dry ingredients, the sour milk, and then the oatmeal.
- Roll the dough out like a pie crust.
- Cut in circles using a drinking glass.
- Bake on a greased cookie sheet at 350° F/180° C for 10-12 minutes.

Date Filling

2 cups	dates	500 mL
$\frac{1}{4}$ cup	brown sugar	50 mL
$\frac{1}{2}$ cup	water	125 mL

- Cook ingredients in a saucepan until the mixture is soft.
- Layer between two oatmeal cookies.

Recipe Hints

The current interest in oat bran makes oatmeal cookies popular as health cookies. Certainly the oats used, whether oatmeal or rolled oats, retain their original fibre and nutrients.

Oatmeal is difficult to obtain in most stores, having been supplanted in most recipes by rolled oats. This recipe still calls for oatmeal for finer texture. Oatmeal can be obtained at bulk food stores.

These cookies can be eaten as they are or made into layered cookies with a date filling.

The clocking girls at the Mercury Mills, Hamilton, 1921. Grandmother Kettle is pictured at lower left and Aunt Bessie at lower right. The women did "clocking" (fancy work) on the sides of stockings. They worked from 7 a.m. to 5 p.m., six days a week, for about $10 per week.

Peanut Butter Cookies

1 cup	peanut butter	250 mL
½ cup	butter	125 mL
1 cup	brown sugar	250 mL
1 cup	Five Roses flour	250 mL
1 tsp	baking soda	5 mL
1	egg	
1 tbsp	vanilla	15 mL
½ tsp	salt	2 mL

- Combine the ingredients in the order stated above.
- Drop spoonfuls of the dough onto a cookie sheet.
- Flatten each spoonful with a fork.
- Bake at 350° F/180° C for 10-15 minutes.

Recipe Hints

Peanut butter cookies are a favourite with all generations. Easy to make, they are the starter recipe for young children wishing to learn to cook. And of course the product is then the property of the child who did the work.

I believe that it was Grandmother's way of ensuring that each child checked in after school. If there was no time for the child to cook on a given day, then a plate of cookies would be waiting to be shared by all. It was not long before playmates wanted to join in on the treats — which increased the pressure to get home quickly.

Grandmother was always very particular about the ingredients which went into each recipe. Peanut butter was as natural as you could get — none of this homogenized product. Today we purchase peanut butter freshly ground at the bulk food or health food store. Only occasionally do we get chunky peanut butter, because the recipe requires ¼ cup more chunky peanut butter.

Butter in all recipes should be softened but not melted.

Peanut Butter Balls

2 tbsp	melted butter	30 mL
1 cup	peanut butter	250 mL
1 cup	icing sugar	250 mL
1 cup	walnuts (chopped)	250 mL
1 cup	dates (chopped fine)	250 mL
¼ tsp	salt	1 mL
	paraffin wax (about the size of a walnut)	

- Mix the first six ingredients together to form a stiff dough.
- Shape the dough into small balls.
- Chill the balls in the refrigerator.
- Melt the chocolate and mix in the paraffin wax.
- Dip the dough balls into the chocolate and allow them to cool.

Recipe Hints

Use natural peanut butter for best results.

Salt should be used sparingly.

Use 1-ounce squares of semi-sweet baking chocolate. You may need more than the suggested amount.

Be aware that some chocolate chips have paraffin already mixed in.

This recipe is superior when pure chocolate is used.

Peanut butter balls last for a long time when frozen.

Rocks

½ cup	butter	125 mL
1 cup	brown sugar	250 mL
2	eggs	
1 tsp	vanilla	5 mL
2 cups	Five Roses flour	500 mL
1 tsp	baking soda	5 mL
1 tsp	nutmeg	5 mL
1 cup	dates (or currants)	250 mL
½ cup	pecans (chopped)	125 mL

- Cream the butter and the sugar.
- Add the eggs and vanilla.
- Fold in the flour, baking soda and nutmeg.
- Add the dates (or currants) and the pecans.
- Drop onto a cookie sheet.
- Bake at 350° F/180° C for 15-20 minutes.
- These cookies are very similar to Hermits, but they have a firm texture and are more chewy. The dates and pecans add variety.

Recipe Hints

The original handwritten recipe called for the cookies to be baked in a hot oven. Through experimentation, hot has been deciphered to mean preheated 15-20 minutes at 350° F/180° C.

The old cookie sheets were always tin. The newer Teflon-coated trays may work at different temperatures.

The dates should be chopped for best mix. Select dates which are still moist rather than those which have dried out.

Chocolate Pinwheels

1/2 cup	butter	125 mL
1/2 cup	sugar	125 mL
1	egg yolk	
1 1/2 cups	Five Roses flour	375 mL
1 tsp	baking powder	5 mL
1 tsp	salt	5 mL
3 tbsp	milk	45 mL
1 square	chocolate (unsweetened)	

- Cream the butter and sugar thoroughly. Add the egg yolk and mix well.
- Sift flour once, measure, then add the baking powder and salt. Sift again.
- Add the flour alternately with the milk. Divide the dough into two equal portions. To one portion add the chocolate and blend. Chill until cool enough to roll flat. Roll each half 1/8" thick.
- Place the plain layer over the chocolate layer and roll them like a jelly roll.
- Chill overnight or until firm enough to slice.
- Cut into 1/8"-thick slices.
- Bake at 400° F/205° C for 5 minutes.

Mexican Wedding Cakes

1 cup	butter	250 mL
4 tbsp	sugar	60 mL
2 cups	Five Roses flour	500 mL
1 cup	walnuts (chopped)	250 mL
1 tbsp	vanilla	15 mL

- Cream ingredients together in order stated above.
- Roll into small balls.
- Drop on a cookie sheet.
- Bake at 350° F/180° C for 15 minutes.
- Roll in icing sugar when cool.

Walnut Cookies

1 cup	brown sugar	250 mL
1 cup	butter	250 mL
1	egg	
1 cup	walnuts (chopped)	250 mL
1 tsp	vanilla	5 mL
½ tsp	baking soda	2 mL
1 tsp	cream of tartar	5 mL
2 cups	Five Roses flour	500 mL

- Cream softened butter with sugar.
- Add egg, dry ingredients and walnuts.
- Roll dough ¼" thick. Cut into cookie shapes.
- Bake at 350° F/180° C for 10-12 minutes.

Banana Nut Cake

²⁄₃ cup	butter	150 mL
1²⁄₃ cups	sugar	400 mL
2¹⁄₂ cups	Swan's Down cake flour	625 mL
1¹⁄₄ tsp	baking powder	6 mL
1 tsp	salt	5 mL
1¹⁄₄ cups	bananas	300 mL
²⁄₃ cup	buttermilk	150 mL
2	eggs	
²⁄₃ cup	walnuts (chopped)	150 mL

- Cream the butter with the sugar.
- Add the dry ingredients.
- Add the bananas and half the buttermilk.
- Mix vigorously for 2 minutes.
- Add the remaining buttermilk and eggs, mix again. Fold in the walnuts. Mix gently.
- Bake in two 9"x2" round pans, lined with paper, at 350° F/ 180° C for 30-35 minutes.

Banana Frosting

¹⁄₃ cup	butter	75 mL
4 cups	icing sugar	1 L
1	egg yolk	
3 tbsp	bananas (ripe, mashed)	45 mL
1 tsp	lemon juice	5 mL

- Mix all ingredients.

Recipe Hints

This is a favourite birthday cake usually served with ice cream.

Bananas are best when ripe to overripe. Overripe bananas can be frozen and saved for this cake or banana muffins.

A picnic at Queenston Heights. Back row, left to right: Bessie Gillespie, Mrs. Sharp, Jessie Fairholme. Front row: Meg Fairholme, Grandmother Kettle, Great-grandmother Gillespie. Grandfather Gillespie worked as a journeyman stonemason at Sharp's Cut Stone in Hamilton.

The Gillespie back yard in Hamilton. From left to right: Aunt Bessie, Uncle Stanley (age 3) and Grandmother Kettle (age 17).

Cherry Cake

1 cup	butter	250 mL
1¾ cups	sugar	425 mL
5	eggs	
3 cups	Five Roses flour	725 mL
¾ tsp	baking powder	3 mL
3 cups	maraschino cherries	725 mL

- Cream the butter and the sugar.
- Add the eggs.
- Mix the sifted flour with the baking powder.
- Add to the butter mixture.
- Fold in the whole cherries.
- Bake in a greased and floured loaf pan at 300° F/150° C for 2½-3 hours.

Recipe Hints

At one time soda crackers were sold in tin boxes. Grandmother used one of these boxes as the size for her cherry cake. A square cake pan is best.

Be sure to drain the juice off the cherries before using. Do not put the cherries into the mixer. Drop them into the finished batter and mix by hand or they will all go to the bottom.

Chiffon Cake

2¼ cups	Swan's Down cake flour	550 mL
1 tsp	baking powder	5 mL
1 tsp	salt	5 mL
1½ cups	sugar	375 mL
½ cup	salad oil	125 mL
6	egg yolks (save the whites)	
¾ cup	cold water	175 mL
2 tsp	lemon juice	10 mL
1 tsp	lemon rind	5 mL
1 tsp	cream of tartar	5 mL

- Mix together the sifted flour, baking powder, salt and sugar.
- Add the salad oil, egg yolks, cold water, lemon juice and lemon rind.
- Mix until smooth.
- Beat the egg whites and cream of tartar together until stiff.
- Fold the flour mixture gently into the egg whites until all is blended. *Do not mix with the Mixmaster.*
- Bake in a greased and floured angel food cake tin at 325° F/-165° C for 60 minutes.

Recipe Hints

A good cake on its own, but Grandmother used to serve it with preserved fruit such as peaches or pears.

One of the biggest seasonal tasks involved most of the family in preserving fruit. Over 200 Mason jars of peaches, pears and raspberries were prepared for winter use.

Grandfather had constructed a cold storage room in the basement, where all of the preserves were stacked on shelves. There was no central heat in the basement, which meant that the temperature stayed around 50° F all year — a perfect temperature for storing preserves and winter vegetables. Buying fruits and vegetables during the Canadian winter was very expensive, when they were available.

The original recipe called for the cook to "make a well in the middle of the dry ingredients and then to add the liquids."
This was a necessary step before the days of the electric mixer. The "well" enabled the cook to gradually bring the dry ingredients into the mix and ensure that all the mix became moist.

Dark Christmas Cake

1½ cups	butter	375 mL
2 cups	brown sugar	500 mL
2 tbsp	vanilla	30 mL
10	eggs	
1 cup	brandy (or rum)	250 mL
½ cup	molasses	125 mL
2 cups	raisins	500 mL
2 cups	currants	500 mL
2 cups	dates (chopped fine)	500 mL
½ cup	black walnuts (chopped)	125 mL
½ cup	mixed peel	125 mL
2 cups	glazed cherries (halved)	500 mL
½ tsp	cloves	2 mL
1 tsp	allspice	5 mL
1 tsp	mace	5 mL
1 tsp	pastry spice (mixed spice)	5 mL
5 cups	Five Roses flour	1¼ L
¾ tsp	baking soda	3 mL

- Cream butter with the sugar in a large bowl.
- Add the eggs, vanilla, molasses and brandy.
- Mix a cup of the flour with the soda and the spices, to be mixed with the dried fruit and nuts.
- Combine the flour with the dried fruit and nuts. Add the floured fruit to the liquid mix.
- The batter will fit into two 8"x8"x3½" cake pans.
- Bake at 275° F/135° C for 3½-4 hours, depending on the size of the pans. Check the cooking by probing the dough with a dry toothpick. When the cakes are cooked, the pick should emerge damp but with no cake dough attached.

Recipe Hints

Blend all the dry ingredients together to ensure they are well mixed. Do the same with all of the liquid components and then mix the two batches.

The Christmas cake has always been Dad's task. The dough, with all of its fruit, is very heavy and requires a large mixing bowl. We use a large stainless-steel salad bowl. The average mixing bowl is too small.

Dad used to collect wild black walnuts for this cake. The outer green husk is removed and the walnuts allowed to dry. The walnut meat should be removed from the cracked shells and placed on a large cookie tray. Dry the meat in the oven and

store in sealed jars. The walnut meat keeps for years if frozen. Use rubber gloves when working with black walnuts. The walnut stain will discolour your hands.

This cake should be made at least 3 months before use. Orange juice may be substituted for the brandy or rum.

Allow the cakes to cool overnight. Wrap them in a double layer of wax paper and a layer of aluminium foil. Store in a cool place.

Treating the Cake

This process is repeated every 2 or 3 weeks or until the cake is all gone. Unwrap the cakes and pour a small amount of a 50-50 mixture of sherry and rum over the cakes. The idea is to moisten the cake, not drench it.

Rewrap the cakes and store in a cool place. The cake can be frozen for storage.

When ready to serve, top the cake with an almond paste (see below) and a layer of white frosting.

Makes about 10 pounds of cake.

Almond Paste

1 cup	ground blanched almonds	250 mL
2 cups	icing sugar	500 mL
1 tsp	vanilla	5 mL
1	egg	

- Combine almonds, ½ sugar, vanilla and the egg. Mix until soft consistency is achieved.
  Add the remaining sugar until the paste is moderately stiff.

Recipe Hints

The paste is used to decorate the Christmas cake. A thick layer, ³⁄₈ " to ½", is placed on a cake and then a layer of frosting over all.

At Christmas, we used to eat a piece of the cake from the bottom, saving the almond paste till last.

Grandmother Kettle (age 8) and sister Bessie (with doll). Notice the fancy laced dresses, even on the doll.

Elizabeth Cake

- Prepare the dates:

1 cup	dates	250 mL
1 cup	boiling water	250 mL
1 tsp	baking soda	5 mL

- Pour the water over the dates and soda. Cook until the dates are soft.

$\frac{1}{4}$ cup	butter	50 mL
1 cup	brown sugar	250 mL
1	egg	
1 tsp	vanilla	5 mL
$1\frac{1}{2}$ cups	Five Roses cake flour	375 mL
1 tsp	baking powder	5 mL
$\frac{1}{2}$ tsp	salt	2 mL
$\frac{1}{2}$ cup	walnuts (chopped)	125 mL

- Cream the butter, sugar, egg and vanilla.
- Add the dry ingredients, the walnuts and the date mix.
- Bake in a $11\frac{1}{2}$"x$7\frac{1}{2}$" cake pan at 350° F/180° C for 30 minutes.

Topping

2 tbsp	cream	30 mL
3 tbsp	butter	45 mL
5 tbsp	brown sugar	75 mL
1 cup	coconut (fine)	250 mL

- Mix together, spread on the warm cake, and brown under the broiler.

Ginger Cake

½ cup	butter	125 mL
½ cup	sugar	125 mL
¼ cup	molasses	50 mL
½ cup	corn syrup	125 mL
2	eggs	
2 cups	Monarch cake and pastry flour	500 mL
1 tsp	baking soda	5 mL
1 tsp	ginger	5 mL
1 tsp	salt	5 mL
½ tsp	cinnamon	2 mL
½ cup	milk	125 mL

- Cream the butter with the sugar.
- Add the molasses, corn syrup, eggs and mix thoroughly.
- Sift and measure the flour separately.
- Add the soda, salt, ginger and cinnamon to the flour and sift again.
- Add the dry ingredients alternately with the milk to the butter mix.
- Mix again.
- Pour into a buttered and floured 9"x9"x2" baking pan.
- Bake at 350° F/180° C for 45 minutes.

Recipe Hints

We have fond memories of Grandmother's hot ginger cake fresh out of the oven, smothered with whipped cream. Certainly not a diet item, but the taste is out of this world.

The original recipe calls for the use of "treacle" rather than molasses. This is an old Scottish term for molasses, which easily substitutes in the recipe.

If you really like ginger use a tablespoon of ginger rather than a teaspoon.

Golden Layer Cake

½ cup	butter	125 mL
2¼ cups	Swan's Down cake flour	550 mL
1½ cups	sugar	375 mL
2 tsp	baking powder	10 mL
1 tsp	salt	5 mL
1 cup	milk	250 mL
2	eggs	
1½ tsp	vanilla	7 mL

- Cream butter to soften.
- Sift in dry ingredients.
- Add ⅔ cup of milk.
- Mix vigorously for 2 minutes until all the flour is moist.
- Add the remaining milk, eggs and vanilla.
- Mix vigorously for 2 minutes longer.
- Pour into two 9"x1½" round cake pans.
- Bake at 350° F/180° C for 30 minutes.

Lemon Filling

¾ cup	sugar	175 mL
2 tbsp	cornstarch	30 mL
¼ tsp	salt	1 mL
1	egg yolk (slightly beaten)	
¾ cup	water	175 mL
3 tbsp	lemon juice	45 mL
1 tsp	lemon rind (grated)	5 mL
1 tbsp	butter	15 mL

- Mix the sugar, cornstarch and salt.
- Add the egg yolk, water and lemon juice.
- Cook in double boiler until thick, stirring constantly.
- Remove from heat, add the lemon peel and the butter.
- Cool the filling before spreading on the bottom layer.
- Place the second layer on top and frost.
- Frost the cake with Chocolate Butter Creamy Frosting (see page 42).

Recipe Hints

If using non-Teflon baking pans, line them with baker's paper for easy removal of cakes.

Lightly grease and flour Teflon pans.

A double boiler is essential to cook the filling but avoid burning.

Grandmother acquired an automatic-stir sauce pot which constantly stirs the mixture while it is cooking. The double boiler has not been used since.

As chief stonemason, Grandfather Alex Gillespie worked on the restoration of Old Fort Henry in Kingston.

Madeira Cake

1 cup	butter	250 mL
2 cups	sugar	500 mL
$\frac{1}{2}$ cup	boiling water	125 mL
3 cups	Monarch cake and pastry flour	725 mL
3	eggs	
2 tsp	baking powder	10 mL
$\frac{1}{2}$ cup	milk	125 mL
1 tsp	lemon extract	5 mL

- Cream the butter first, then with the sugar until smooth.
- Add the boiling water slowly, mixing well.
- Add 1 cup of flour, then 1 egg. Mix thoroughly.
- Repeat with second cup of flour and 1 egg.
- After sifting the baking powder into the third cup of flour, repeat the process.
- Add the milk and the lemon extract.
- Bake in a well-greased, deep, round pan at 300° F/150° C for $1\frac{1}{2}$ hours.
- The heat must be even. Too much heat at any one time may result in a damp centre.

Recipe Hints

The flour used in the cake recipes has been specified. Grandmother spent a great deal of time and effort testing cake flours to get the soft, melt-in-your-mouth taste. For general purposes, she used Monarch cake and pastry flour. Even though the flour for the cakes is advertised as pre-sifted, Grandmother would sift the flour to make the cake softer. For really fine cakes, Swan's Down cake flour was her favourite. A firm-textured cake like Madeira required a general-purpose flour.

Light Fruit Cake

1 cup	butter	250 mL
1 1/2 cups	sugar	375 mL
4	eggs	
3 cups	Five Roses flour	725 mL
1/2 tsp	baking powder	2 mL
1/2 tsp	salt	2 mL
2 cups	raisins	500 mL
1 cup	maraschino cherries (cut in half)	250 mL
2 cups	currants	500 mL
	juice and grated rind of 1/2 lemon	

- Cream the butter with the sugar.
- Add the eggs.
- Add the sifted dry ingredients.
- Fold in the fruits.
- Bake at 275° F/135° C for 2 hours in a loaf pan.
- Turn off the heat but leave the cake in the oven for 15 minutes.

Uncle Eric and Grandfather Walter Kettle were always dressed in their best, even on a picnic.

Orange Cake

½ cup	butter	125 mL
1 cup	sugar	250 mL
½ tsp	salt	2 mL
1	egg (beaten)	
¾ cup	milk	175 mL
2 tsp	baking powder	10 mL
2 cups	Five Roses cake flour	500 mL
	juice and grated rind of 1 orange	

- If you prefer, use sour milk. If so, substitute 1 teaspoon baking soda and 1 teaspoon of baking powder for 2 teaspoons baking powder.
- Cream the butter and sugar together.
- Add the beaten egg.
- Sift the flour, salt, soda and baking powder together. Also sift in soda if using sour milk.
- Add the dry ingredients to the milk, the orange rind and the juice.
- Bake in a loaf pan 9"x5"x3" at 350° F/180° C for 35 minutes.
- Frost with an orange frosting (use lemon/orange recipe).

Recipe Hints

Uncle Reg raved about this cake. He would eat an entire cake at one sitting if no one was watching.

Sour milk can be made by adding 1 teaspoon of vinegar to a cup of milk. Sour the milk before you start mixing the other ingredients.

Sour milk was quite common before the days of refrigerators. Cooks found many ways to make use of this milk.

Pound Cake

1 cup	butter	250 mL
1⅔ cups	sugar	400 mL
5	eggs	
2 cups	Five Roses cake flour or	500 mL
	Monarch cake and pastry flour	

- Cream the butter, mix in the sugar and the eggs, one at a time.
- When creamy, fold in the flour
- Pour into a buttered and floured 9"x5" bread pan.
- Bake at 300° F/150° C for 1¾ hours.

Recipe Hints

Butter is the characteristic flavour of this cake, but you may like to add a tablespoon of brandy or lemon juice for flavour.

The cake improves in flavour and texture when stored for a day or two before eating.

This is a great loaf cake for after activities.

*Phillip Kettle (age 2½)
in the back yard on
Edgemont in Hamilton.*

Sour Cream Fudge Cake

2 cups	Swan's Down cake flour	500 mL
1 tsp	soda	5 mL
1 tsp	salt	5 mL
1½	cups sugar	375 mL
⅓ cup	butter	75 mL
1 cup	sour cream	250 mL
3 squares	chocolate (unsweetened)	
2	eggs	
1 tsp	vanilla	5 mL
¼ cup	hot water	50 mL

- Sift the flour, then measure.
- Sift together the sifted cake flour, soda, salt and sugar.
- Cream in the butter and sour cream. Mix for 2 minutes, first at low speed then at medium speed.
- Add the melted chocolate, eggs, vanilla and hot water. Mix for 2 minutes.
- Bake in well-greased and lightly floured cake pans at 350° F/-180° C: 8" round layer pans for 30-35 minutes; 9" round layer pans for 25-30 minutes; 13"x9"x2" pan for 35-45 minutes.
- Frost the cake with Chocolate Butter Creamy Frosting (see page 42).

Recipe Hints

At every family birthday, picnic or gathering where food was served, Grandmother's chocolate cake was the first to be eaten. Everyone who was a chocolate freak, or who just liked a good piece of cake, came back for seconds. Then tragedy struck. Grandmother lost the recipe. It was at least 10 years before the recipe reappeared. The sour cream fudge cake was the prized recipe.

Swan's Down cake flour is the flour Grandmother always chose for layer cakes. There was a period of time when she was unable to find this flour in local stores. During that time she used Five Roses cake flour or Monarch cake flour, but continually lamented on her inability to locate her preferred flour.

Sponge Cake

1 cup	sugar	250 mL
4	eggs (separated)	
1 cup	Monarch cake and pastry flour	250 mL
2 tsp	baking powder	10 mL

- Cream sugar and the egg yolks.
- Add the sifted dry ingredients.
- Beat the egg whites until they are stiff.
- Fold egg whites into the cake batter lightly by hand.
- Bake in two 8" round cake pans at 300° F/150° C for 30-35 minutes.

Recipe Hints

This cake recipe came into use during the strawberry and raspberry seasons. The cake has very little flavour of its own. Its main function is to soak up the juices of the berries and the melted ice cream.

This cake is definitely best when used fresh. It should be made with only enough time for it to cool before using.

Swan's Down Butter Cake

½ cup	butter	125 mL
1 cup	sugar	250 mL
2 cups	Swan's Down cake flour	500 mL
3 tsp	baking powder	15 mL
⅓ cup	milk	75 mL
1 tsp	vanilla	5 mL
3	egg whites (whisked)	

- Cream butter until light and fluffy.
- Add the sugar gradually, creaming together thoroughly.
- Sift flour once and measure.
- Add baking powder and sift again.
- Add the sifted flour mixture alternately with the milk, a small amount at a time. Mix thoroughly.
- Add vanilla.
- Fold in the egg whites.
- Bake in a large greased and floured pan or in layers. Large pan: 350° F/180° C for 30-35 minutes. Layer pans: 375° F/190° C for 20-25 minutes.
- Frost with the butter frosting used on the Mystery Cake.

Recipe Hints

Sifting the flour loosens it, as it tends to compact after sitting for a long time. It is necessary to sift first before attempting to measure accurately.

Luscious Lemon Frosting

1 tbsp	grated orange rind	15 mL
3 tbsp	butter	45 mL
3 cups	icing sugar (sifted)	725 mL
2 tbsp	lemon juice	30 mL
3 tbsp	water	45 mL
1/8 tsp	salt	1/2 mL

- Cream the orange rind with the butter; add the sugar gradually, mixing well after each addition.
- Combine lemon juice and water.
- Add to the creamed mixture alternately with remaining sugar until the frosting reaches a smooth spreading consistency.
- Add the salt. Mix again.
- Makes enough frosting to cover a two-layer 9" cake or one 13"x9"x2" cake generously.

Recipe Hint

The frosting is at a suitable consistency when it spreads over the cake without pulling the cake to pieces or soaking into the cake.

A wet table knife will put a smooth surface on the frosting if required.

Note: Add orange juice (for flavouring) instead of lemon for a delicious orange frosting.

Orange rind gives the icing more colour. You can also use lemon or lime if you like.

Before emigrating from England, Great-grandmother Kettle operated her own business as a women's tailor.

Grandmother Kettle made the suits worn by Phillip and Lois Kettle in this photograph.

Easy Penuche Icing

½ cup	butter	125 mL
1 cup	brown sugar	250 mL
¼ cup	milk	50 mL
1¾ cups	icing sugar	425 mL

- Melt butter in a saucepan. Add brown sugar and milk.
- Cook over low heat for 2 minutes, stirring constantly.
- Cool to lukewarm.
- Gradually add icing sugar. Mix until thick enough to spread.
- If icing becomes too stiff, add a little hot water.

Recipe Hints

This icing provides a change from white icing on plain cakes.

Creamy Chocolate Frosting

Sufficient to ice a two-layer cake

5 squares	Baker's semi-sweet chocolate	
3 cups	icing sugar	725 mL
¼ tsp	salt	1 mL
2½ tbsp	hot water	40 mL
⅓ cup	butter	75 mL
1	egg	
½ tsp	vanilla	2 mL

- Heat the chocolate until melted.
- Add half the sugar, salt and water. Mix well.
- Add the butter a little at a time, stirring constantly.
- Add the remaining sugar alternately with the egg.
- Add the vanilla. Mix well.
- Cool before spreading.

Caramel Squares

Bottom Layer

½ cup	butter	125 mL
1	egg yolk	
¾ cup	brown sugar	175 mL
1 tsp	vanilla	5 mL
1½ cups	Monarch cake and pastry flour	375 mL
1 tsp	baking powder	5 mL

- Cream the butter, egg yolk, brown sugar and vanilla.
- Add the dry ingredients.
- Spread into a 9"x9" baking pan. Pack firmly.

Filling

1	egg white (beaten stiff)	
¾ cup	brown sugar	175 mL
¾ cup	chopped walnuts	175 mL

- Fold together the ingredients. Spread over the bottom layer.
- Bake at 350° F/180° C for 25-30 minutes.

Recipe Hints

Whenever Caramel Squares and Mystery Cake were served at the same time, a contest developed to see who could eat the most. To my knowledge no one ever decided which was the better eating.

Caramel Squares are a great dessert item just by themselves. They can also be served in larger squares with ice cream and caramel sauce.

Do not beat the egg whites with the electric mixer because it makes the filling too stiff. Use a hand beater or a whisk.

Add the brown sugar slowly and then add the walnuts. Continue to mix but do not over mix.

Chocolate Dream Cake (Brownies)

½ cup	butter (melted)	125 mL
1 cup	brown sugar	250 mL
¾ cup	walnuts (chopped)	175 mL
¼ cup	coconut (fine, unsweetened)	50 mL
1	egg	
2 tbsp	cocoa	30 mL
1 tsp	vanilla	5 mL
½ cup	Monarch cake and pastry flour	125 mL
¼ tsp	salt	1 mL

- Add the ingredients to the melted butter in the order stated above.
- Put the mix into an 8"x8"x2" cake pan.
- Cook at 350° F/180° C for 25 minutes.

Chocolate Butter Creamy Frosting

¾ cup	cocoa	175 mL
2⅔ cup	icing sugar	650 mL
6 tbsp	butter	90 mL
6 tbsp	milk	90 mL
1 tsp	vanilla	5 mL

- Combine sugar and cocoa in a bowl.
- Cream the butter with half the cocoa mixture in a second bowl.
- Add the remaining cocoa mixture alternately with milk.
- Mix until icing attains spreading consistency.
- Blend in the vanilla.
- Spread over cool cake.

Recipe Hints

These brownies are the result of experimenting with several other recipes which did not come up to standard. It is another square to be served with Caramel Squares and the Mystery Cake. An absolutely decadent dessert when served with ice cream and chocolate sauce.

Mix the ingredients in a large cooking pot on the stove.

Melt the butter at a low heat.

Take the butter off the heat and add the remaining ingredients. Allow the cake to cool before attempting to ice it.

Coconut Graham Squares

Bottom Layer

$1/4$ cup	butter (melted)	50 mL
2 cups	graham cracker crumbs (fine)	500 mL
$7/8$ of the can	sweetened condensed milk	200 mL
1 cup	coconut (fine)	250 mL

- Combine melted butter and crushed crumbs.
- Press into an 8"x8"x2" cake pan.
- Bake at 350° F/180° C for 5 minutes.

Filling

- Mix the sweetened condensed milk and the coconut.
- Spread on top of the graham cracker base.
- Bake until brown at 350° F/180° C for 25 minutes.

Cocoa Butter Frosting

$2^{1}/_{2}$ cups	icing sugar	625 mL
$1/4$ cup	cocoa	50 mL
$1/8$ tsp	salt	$1/2$ mL
$1/3$ cup	butter	75 mL
3 tbsp	cream (hot)	45 mL
1	egg yolk	
1 tsp	vanilla	5 mL

- Sift together the sugar and the cocoa.
- Cream the butter with the cream, sugar, cocoa and salt.
- Add the egg yolk and the vanilla. Blend thoroughly.
- Spread the icing when the cake is cool.

Recipe Hints

Grandmother preferred to make her own graham cracker crumbs from the whole crackers rather than purchase the prepared crumbs. Twenty-six crackers will make 2 cups of crumbs. Her children are lazy, so tend to buy the cracker crumbs already crushed.

The old house at the corner of Appleby Line and Lakeshore Highway in 1935. Before any of the modern development took place, Burlington extended only one block east of Brant Street. The Kettles lived in this house for one winter.

Camping 1928 style: Grandmother Kettle, Grandfather Kettle and the Ackeroyds.

Date Squares

Bottom Layer

1 cup	butter	250 mL
1 cup	brown sugar	250 mL
2 cups	rolled oats (regular)	500 mL
1½ cups	Five Roses flour	375 mL
½ tsp	baking soda	2 mL
1 tsp	baking powder	5 mL

- Cream the butter and the sugar.
- Add the dry ingredients gradually while mixing.
- Spread half the mixture on the bottom of a 10" baking pan.

Filling

2 cups	dates	500 mL
¼ cup	brown sugar	50 mL
½ cup	water	125 mL

- Put the dates, water and sugar into a pan and cook slowly until the dates are soft. Keep a lid on the pan for better steaming.
- Spread the date mixture on top of the bottom layer of rolled oats.
- Allow to cool and stiffen.
- Spread the remaining oat mixture on top.
- Cook at 375° F/190° C for 30-35 minutes.

Recipe Hints

It is always a compliment to have someone ask for your recipe. Recipes were passed through friends and relatives. Date Squares came from Grandmother's sister's sister-in-law.

Dates take longer to cool than does the bottom layer, so Grandmother always made the filling first. It would then be cool when put onto the bottom oatmeal layer.

Don't buy dates which feel too dry. They are difficult to work with and require more water for the correct consistency. Buying the dates in bulk food stores enables you to pick dates which are moist. Honey dates add to the taste but are more expensive to use.

Mystery Cake Squares

Bottom Layer

½ cup	butter	125 mL
1 cup	Monarch cake and pastry flour	250 mL

- Cream ingredients together. Spread in a 9" cake pan. Bake at 350° F/180° C for 20 minutes.

Filling

1 cup	brown sugar	250 mL
1 cup	coconut (fine)	250 mL
½ cup	walnuts (fine)	125 mL
2	eggs	
1 tbsp	vanilla	15 mL
1 tsp	baking powder	5 mL

- Mix all the ingredients together and spread them on the pre-cooked pastry. Bake until brown at 350° F/180° C for 20 minutes.
- Cool.
- Cover with Butter Frosting. Chill for 24 hours before cutting.

Butter Frosting

⅓ cup	butter	75 mL
4 cups	icing sugar (sifted)	1 L
1	egg yolk (optional)	
1 tsp	vanilla	5 mL
2½ tbsp	cream	40 mL

- Mix ingredients and spread evenly over the cake.

Recipe Hints

This recipe came from a church bazaar in Hamilton, Ontario, during the 1930s. Patrons of the bazaar were given a taste of the squares and then were asked to purchase the recipe for a dime – an interesting way for a church group to raise money. Naturally the price would need to be updated.

These squares are a favourite with anyone who tries them.

Cook on a shelf at mid-oven, not on the bottom shelf.

If cream is not available for the frosting, use milk.

It is a good practice to allow the bottom layer to cool before adding the filling. Allow the filling to cool before icing the squares. If the cake is not allowed to cool, the shortbread bottom will stick to the pan when cut.

If you are in a hurry it is possible to make the filling while the bottom layer is cooking. Gently spoon the filling onto the bottom layer. Spread carefully.

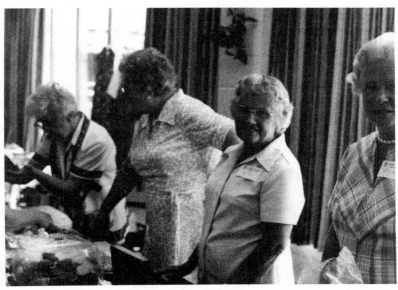

A bake sale at First Place retirement apartments. Grandmother's goodies were always in demand and often the first to be sold.

Raspberry Bars

Bottom Layer

1 cup	Monarch cake and pastry flour	250 mL
1/8 tsp	salt	1 1/2 mL
1 tsp	baking powder	5 mL
1	egg	
1/2 cup	butter	125 mL
1 tbsp	milk	15 mL

- Mix the flour, salt and baking powder together.
- Fold in the egg, butter and milk.
- Spread into an 8"x8"x2" cake pan with the mix.
- Spread the dough with a generous layer of raspberry jam.

Topping

1	egg	
1 cup	sugar	250 mL
1/2 tsp	vanilla	2 mL
1/3 cup	butter	75 mL
2 cups	coconut (fine)	500 mL

- Mix the ingredients thoroughly.
- Spread on top of the jam.
- Bake the squares at 350° F/180° C for 40 minutes.
- Cut into squares after the cake has been allowed to cool.

Recipe Hints

The best flavour for raspberry bars is attained by using real homemade jam with no added pectin. If you are too busy, someone else's homemade jam can be obtained at a farmers' market.

Raspberry Jam

2 cups	raspberries	500 mL
2 cups	sugar	500 mL

- Mix the berries and the sugar in a pot
- Bring to a low simmering boil until the mix stiffens (20 minutes).
- Allow to cool before using.

Recipe Hints

A jam can be made by cooking the berry sugar mix in the microwave oven.

To save time and to avoid heating the kitchen during the summer, freeze the raspberries at the peak of the season and make the jam a jar at a time during the winter.

You couldn't picnic all year, so these ladies met at each other's homes for lunch twice a month. Left to right: Meg Moxham, Grandmother Kettle, Jan Grace, Betty Fraser, unknown, Aunt Bessie, Grandmother Gillespie. Photo circa 1936.

Shortbread

2 cups	butter	500 mL
1 cup (heaping)	fruit sugar	250 mL
4 cups	Five Roses flour	1 L

"First Fit"

In the highlands of Scotland, New Year's Eve was once a bigger celebration than Christmas. On New Year's, couples would strive to be the first to visit their neighbours with cake in hand. The first to cross the threshold was guaranteed good fortune for the year to come. Hence the term "first fit" or "first feet" was applied to the lucky couple. The favoured cake was shortbread because it kept well, carried easily and was simple to make.

- Beat the butter until creamy. *Do not melt the butter.*
- Add the sugar while still creaming the butter in the mixer.
- Add the flour a cup at a time, being sure that each cup is well mixed before adding another.
- The dough is of the correct consistency when it can be handled without sticking.
- Place the entire dough onto a cookie sheet and mold into a loaf.
- Cut the loaf into four equal parts.
- Flatten each portion to about $1\frac{1}{4}$" thick.
- Bake at 350° F/180° C for an hour.
- The shortbread is done when it is golden brown.

Recipe Hints

Grandmother always partially cut the loaves to make them easier to serve later. While the shortbread is still warm, make cuts halfway through each loaf in sizes that you would like to serve. The cakes break easily along those lines when they are cold.

Fruit sugar can be obtained at a bulk food store.

Pie Pastry

All of the pies and tarts in this book are based on this pie dough.

2 cups (1 lb)	lard (chilled)	500 mL
4 cups	Five Roses flour	1 L
$\frac{1}{4}$ tsp	salt	1 mL
$\frac{2}{3}$ cups	water (chilled)	150 mL

- Measure the flour and place in the refrigerator until cool to the touch.
- Add the salt before adding the lard.
- Cut lard into pieces. Work well into the flour and salt mixture until it achieves a mealy consistency.
- Add water until dough is workable.
- Using a floured rolling pin, roll out the dough on a piece of floured wax paper.
- Place the dough in a pie plate by turning the wax paper over and positioning the crust in the pie plate.
- The recipe makes sufficient dough for two or three pies. Store what is not used in sealed plastic bags in the freezer for future pies.

Recipe Hints

Grandmother has always been fussy about the use of lard in her pie pastry. Today her brand of lard is Tenderflake.

Working the lard into the flour and salt is crucial. She is an absolute fanatic about having the ingredients ice cold and handling them as little as possible. The heat of the cook's hands can alter the consistency of the dough.

Cold flour and the chilled lard are worked together with a cold table knife.

Shortening can be used in place of lard.

Apple Pie

Use Grandmother's pie crust.

6-7	apples (good-sized)	
3/4 cup	sugar	175 mL
2 tbsp	flour	30 mL
2 tbsp	butter	30 mL

- Peel, core and cut the apples into small slices.
- Combine the apples, sugar and flour.
- Put into the uncooked pie crust.
- Place a few small pieces of butter on the apples.
- Cover with a second crust.
- Crimp the edges of the pie.
- Bake at mid-level of a preheated oven.
- Cook at 450° F/230° C for 20 minutes, then at 425° F/215° C for 25 minutes or until the pie is brown.

Recipe Hints

The key to a good apple pie lies in the apples. They should be a little tart in taste for best results.

Many of the best pie apples have been replaced in orchards by apples which store better and can be transported with less damage. Gravensteen apples make prize-winning pies. Unfortunately the fruit does not keep more than a few weeks before it begins to deteriorate. You may be assured that the existence of a Gravensteen tree is known to local pie makers.

The transparent apple is another disappearing favourite. This apple is picked in late July and early August, while it is green but just beginning to turn yellow.

Our favourite of the available apples is the Spy, either Northern or Red.

Blueberry Pie

2½ cups	blueberries	625 mL
½ cup	sugar	125 mL
2 tbsp	flour	30 mL
¼ tsp	lemon juice	1 mL
⅛ tsp	salt	½ mL
1 tbsp	butter	15 mL

- Combine the blueberries with the sugar, flour, lemon juice and salt.
- Place the berry mix in an uncooked pie crust (Grandmother's pie crust).
- Place a few small pieces of butter over the berries.
- Cover with a top crust. Make small slits in the crust to allow the steam to escape.
- Bake at 450° F/230° C for 10 minutes, then at 375° F/190° C for 25 minutes or until the crust is brown and the berries are tender.
- If desired, a glaze may be applied to the crust before cooking. Brush the crust with "top milk" and sprinkle sugar lightly and evenly over it. The baking will melt the sugar. Ten percent cream can be used instead of top milk.

Recipe Hints

Much of the good taste of a blueberry pie comes from the picking of the berries. We have many fond memories of picking, cooking and eating these pies.

Wild blueberries may or may not be the best tasting, depending on the season. Dry weather seems to result in poor-quality berries.

Top Milk

Many in the younger generation will not know this term. At one time dairies like Silverwoods delivered milk in narrow-necked bottles to homes. The top of the bottle contained rich cream. By using a special spoon to block the narrow neck of the bottle, mothers were able to pour off the cream for a variety of uses. The milk just below the cream had a butterfat content much like 10% or 18% table creams. This was called top milk. It was valued for coffee and for hot cereals.

Children loved the cold winter morning delivery of the cream-top bottles. The cold froze the milk, causing the cream to expand and pop the cap. The resulting extrusion of frozen cream tasted like ice cream. We would take the cream and eat it on the way to school. We always put the lid back on the bottle with the mistaken idea that no one would notice the loss.

On the swing in Grandfather Gillespie's yard in Hamilton. Left to right: Phillip Kettle, Grandfather Walter Kettle and Lois Pounder (Kettle).

Butterscotch Pie

Filling

1 cup	brown sugar	250 mL
1/3 cup	cornstarch	75 mL
1/4 tsp	salt	1 mL
1 cup	boiling water	250 mL
1 1/2 cups	milk (heated)	375 mL
2	eggs (separated)	
1/2 tsp	vanilla	2 mL
4 tbsp	icing sugar	60 mL

- Precook a pie crust until it is light tan in colour (400° F/ 205° C) for 15-20 minutes.
- In a saucepan, combine the brown sugar, cornstarch and salt.
- Add 1 cup of boiling water, cook at low heat, stirring constantly until mixture thickens.
- Add beaten egg yolks and milk.
- Stir until thick.
- Remove saucepan from heat.
- Add the vanilla.
- Pour the filling into a precooked pie shell.
- Top with meringue, made with whipped egg whites and icing sugar.
- Bake for 10-12 minutes at 400° F/205° C.

Recipe Hints

An all-time favourite dessert pie. Basically a pie shell with butterscotch pudding topped with a meringue.

Prick the bottom crust with a fork before baking to avoid having the crust bubble up as the butterscotch is poured into the shell.

To stop the filling from breaking the crust as you pour it in, pour over a spoon.

Boston Cream Pie

The Cake Layers

2	eggs (separated)	
½ cup	cold water	125 mL
1 cup	sugar (fine)	250 mL
1 cup	Monarch cake flour	250 mL
¾ tsp	baking powder	3 mL
¼ tsp	salt	1 mL
1 tsp	vanilla	5 mL
¼ tsp	lemon juice	1 mL

- Beat the egg whites until stiff, then set aside.
- Beat the water and the egg yolks until very light and fluffy, and tripled in volume.
- Add the sugar 2 tablespoons at a time, mixing well after each addition. Continue to mix until thick and lemon coloured.
- Sift flour, baking powder and salt together; gently stir into egg mixture.
- Add flavourings. Fold in the stiffly beaten egg whites.
- Pour batter into two 8" layer pans lined with waxed paper and greased.
- Bake at 350° F/180° C for 25-30 minutes.
- Cool the layers completely in the pans before trying to remove them.
- Remove layers from pans and spread the cream filling between them.

Cream Filling

2 cups	milk	500 mL
6 tbsp	flour	90 mL
½ cup	sugar	125 mL
¾ tsp	salt	3 mL
3	eggs	
2 tbsp	butter	30 mL
2 tsp	vanilla	10 mL

- Scald milk in a double boiler.
- Combine the flour, salt, butter and sugar.
- Add a little scalded milk, stir constantly.
- Return all to the double boiler.
- Cook over hot water until smooth and thick.

- Combine the lightly beaten eggs and the remaining $\frac{1}{4}$ cup of sugar. Slowly stir into the milk mixture.
- Return to the double boiler. Cook 5 minutes longer, stirring. Remove from heat. Add flavourings just before spreading the cream onto the cakes.

Grandmother Kettle dressed for the winter of 1923.

Custard Pie

2 cups	scalded milk	500 mL
1/2 cup	sugar	125 mL
4	eggs (lightly beaten)	

- Prepare an uncooked pie shell.
- Beat the eggs until well mixed but not frothy.
- Add the sugar to the milk.
- Slowly add the milk mix to the eggs, stirring constantly.
- Pour the custard mix slowly into the uncooked deep pie shell. A frozen pie shell can be used.
- Sprinkle nutmeg over the surface.
- Cook at 400° F/205° C for 15 minutes.
- Lower heat to 300° F/150° C for 15 minutes.
- To ensure it has set, test pie by giving it a mild shake.

Coconut Custard Topping For Custard Pie

1/4 cup	coconut (fine)	50 mL
2 tbsp	brown sugar	30 mL
1 tbsp	butter (soft)	15 mL

- Combine the ingredients and sprinkle over the baked custard pie.
- Broil until the coconut is brown.

Recipe Hints

Pouring the custard into the pie shell often results in a hole in the shell. The shell may then "float" into the custard. To avoid this, use a frozen pastry shell or pour the mixture over a spoon.

Fresh Jack-O'-Lantern Pie

1 1/2 cups	pumpkin	375 mL
1 cup	brown sugar	250 mL
1/2 tsp	cinnamon	2 mL
1/2 tsp	nutmeg	2 mL
1/2 tbsp	molasses	8 mL
1 tsp	ginger	5 mL
1/2 tsp	salt	2 mL
1 cup	milk	250 mL
2	eggs	

- Blend all ingredients and pour into an uncooked pastry shell. Cook at 450° F/230° C for 15 minutes; then at 400° F/205° C for 45 minutes.
- Serve warm or cold.

Recipe Hints

In our household the Halloween pumpkin didn't go into the garbage after the witches and goblins night; it was used to make pies. In fact one or two extra pumpkins were purchased to be prepared and frozen for winter use.

Squash blended in with the pumpkin will give the flesh a smooth, even texture.

This pie should be served with a liberal amount of whipped cream.

Prepare Your Own Pumpkin

Place a medium-sized pumpkin in a roasting pan and puncture it with a sharp knife.

Bake the pumpkin in the oven at 350° F/180° C until the gourd is soft.

A large pumpkin can be cut in half and cooked face down.

Cut the pumpkin open when soft, remove the seeds and discard them.

Scoop out the flesh and put into the food processor. Mix vigorously to break up the fibres.

Pour off any excess liquid. Put the blended mash into a colander to allow it to drain.

Store in 1 1/2-cup plastic containers until needed. We use recycled cottage cheese containers.

The frozen pumpkin will keep for a long time.

Lemon Chiffon Pie

Lemon Custard

1	precooked pastry shell	
3	egg yolks	
½ cup	sugar	125 mL
	juice and rind of 1 lemon	
3 tbsp	water	45 mL
¼ tsp	salt	1 mL

- Beat the egg yolks in the top of a double boiler, over heat.
- Add sugar, lemon juice, rind, water and salt.
- Cook until the mix is thickened. Stir constantly.
- Remove from the heat.
- Pour the cooled mixture into the pie crust.

Meringue

½ cup	sugar	125 mL
3	egg whites	

- Beat the egg whites and ¼ cup sugar until stiff but not dry.
- Add the second ¼ cup of sugar slowly to the egg whites, beating the mixture well while doing so.
- Fold the custard into the meringue gradually.
- Pour the filling into the pie crust.
- Bake at 325° F/165° C for 20 minutes or until it is set.
- Cool the pie before cutting.

Recipe Hints

The lemon pie filler is the correct consistency when it coats the stir spoon and stays on the spoon.

The double boiler is the traditional way to cook sauces and custards to keep them from burning.

There is a stir pot on the market today which electrically cooks and stirs the sauces without being watched. Grandmother has put her double boiler into storage since she obtained one of these modern devices.

Cool the lemon mixture before pouring it gently into the egg whites.

Strawberry Pie

1 quart box	fresh strawberries (washed and hulled)	
1 cup	sugar	250 mL
2 tbsp	cornstarch (heaping)	30 mL
1	precooked pie crust	

- Mash 1 cup berries. Save the others.
- Add the sugar and cornstarch to the mash.
- In a saucepan, cook the berry mix at medium heat until it is thick and glazed.
- Arrange the whole berries in the pie shell. Pour the cooked berries over them.
- Allow the pie to cool, then serve with whipped cream.

Glaze for Fresh Fruit Pies

¾ cup	sugar	175 mL
2½ tbsp	cornstarch	40 mL
¼ tsp	salt	1 mL
1 cup	water	250 mL

- Combine all ingredients in a saucepan.
- Cook until thick, stirring constantly.
- Pour over the berries in the pie crust or mix together with the berries.

Recipe Hints

Grandmother preferred to eat the strawberries with cream or over ice cream. Consequently we seldom had enough berries left for a pie.

Fresh berries picked locally always tasted better than the imported kind.

Coconut Tarts

12	uncooked tart shells	
	red currant jelly	
¼ cup	butter	50 mL
1	egg	
¼ cup	sugar	50 mL
¾ cup	coconut (fine)	175 mL

- Use Grandmother's pie pastry for the tart shells.
- Put 1 teaspoon of red currant jelly into the bottom centre of each uncooked tart shell.
- Mix the butter, egg, sugar and coconut together.
- Place the mixture gently over the jelly in the tart shells.
- Bake at 450° F/230° C for 12 minutes.

Recipe Hints

The interesting flavour of the coconut tarts is imparted by the homemade red currant jelly. Red currant jelly is not always easy to obtain commercially, but it is not difficult to make. Our whole family is always on the lookout for red currants during the short season in late June.

Red Currant Jelly

- Grandmother used upwards of 12 quarts of fresh red currants to produce an adequate supply of jelly for winter tart production.
- It is best to pick the berries off the stems.
- Cook the berries until the skins begin to break and the berries take on a white cast.
- Add a small amount of water to avoid burning the fruit (about ½ cup).
- To collect the berry juice put the cooked berries into a cheesecloth bag or an old pillow case and allow the juice to drip into a large pot.
- Add 1 cup of sugar to 1 cup of berry juice.
- Bring the sugar and juice to a slow boil, then allow it to cool.
- The jelly can be sealed tightly and stored as a jam or it can be frozen.

Butter Tarts

12	uncooked tart shells	
1 cup	brown sugar	250 mL
2	eggs	
1 cup	currants	250 mL
⅛ cup	butter (softened)	25 mL
1 tsp	vanilla	5 mL
3 tbsp	milk	45 mL

- Mix all the ingredients and put into uncooked tart shells.
- Cook at 450° F/230° C for 10-12 minutes.

Recipe Hints

It was always fun stuffing ourselves with first a coconut tart and then a butter tart, trying to decide which one tasted better. After hundreds of both tarts we still have not decided.

Use a 12-hole tart pan.

Purchase the freshest available currants.

Pecan Tarts

12	uncooked tart shells	
2	eggs	
½ cup	corn syrup	125 mL
½ tsp	vanilla	2 mL
½ cup	brown sugar	125 mL
¼ tsp	salt	1 mL
1 cup	pecans (whole)	250 mL

- Combine the ingredients and pour into the unbaked tart shells.
- Bake at 450° F/230° C for 10-12 minutes.

Chicken Pie

1	6-7 lb roasting chicken	½ kg
2	onions (small)	
2	bay leaves	
4	celery stalks (no tops)	
2	chili peppers (dried)	
3	carrots (cooked)	
2 cups	green peas (cooked, frozen)	500 mL
⅛ tsp	pepper	½ mL
2 tsp	salt	10 mL

- Pie pastry to cover baking dish.
- Cut the chicken into pieces. Wash in cold water.
- Put pieces into a stock pot and cover with boiling water.
- Add the chopped onion, bay leaf, chopped celery and the chili peppers.
- Cover and simmer until the chicken is tender. Add the salt.
- Allow the pot to cool until the chicken can be handled. Remove most of the fat with a metal spoon and set aside.
- Take out the chicken. Heat the stock to a liquid and measure. For each cup of stock, melt 2 tbsp of chicken fat; add 2 tbsp flour and stir until well blended. Add the stock slowly and bring to a boil. Season to taste with salt and pepper.
- Remove skin and debone the chicken.
- Put a "birdie" or an inverted custard cup in the centre of a 14"x12" pyrex casserole dish
- Arrange the pieces of chicken around the birdie.
- Add the cooked carrots and peas.
- Pour the stock sauce over the chicken and the vegetables.
- The mixture should not be more than 2" deep, so that it will heat thoroughly while the pastry bakes.
- Cool the dish to room temperature.
- Roll out the pie pastry. Cut to fit the baking dish. Lay it over the dish so that the birdie holds the crust over the pie.
- Bake for 10 minutes at 450° F/230° C.
- Reduce heat to 350° F/180° C for 15 minutes or until the pastry is a delicate brown.

Recipe Hints

The key to a successful Chicken Pie is the chicken. Grand-mother did not use stewing fowl, which are the oldest birds. She used only the prime, young roasting capons, preferring to buy the 6-7 pound birds from a farmers' market. Two or three smaller birds could be used.

Birdies

It would be interesting to do a historical study on these small pottery items. They are almost impossible to find in a shop in Canada.

The birdie is approximately 3" high, hollow, and shaped like a squat funnel. The wide end is placed down in a baking dish, with the narrow end protruding through the pie crust. It is used to allow the steam of the pie to escape during the cooking.

The name birdie *probably derives from the whistling noise made by the "funnel" as the steam escapes.*

Many other shapes have been available over the years. There is a crow-shaped birdie, a castle and the funnel. A very useful curiosity. We go looking for birdies when we travel in the British Isles.

Grandmother prefers to use fresh carrots, purchased with the tops still on, for more flavour.

Small, delicate frozen peas are acceptable.

A cup of stemmed, sliced fresh mushrooms add flavour to the pie.

Take the chili peppers out of the liquid before you boil down the stock if you prefer a milder flavour.

Grandmother Kettle (age 19) at the reservoir on the side of Hamilton Mountain.

Steak and Kidney Pie

1½ lbs	round steak	⅔ kg
1 lb	beef kidney	½ kg
½ cup	Five Roses flour	125 mL
½ tsp	salt	2 mL
½ tsp	pepper	2 mL
2	big cooking onions (chopped)	
6	carrots	
	boiling water	
	pie pastry sufficient to cover the baking pan	

- Cut the steak and the kidneys into ½" cubes.
- Shake in a bag with flour, salt and pepper.
- Brown in cooking oil in a fry pan.
- Cover with water and add the carrots.
- Add the onions to the pot.
- Simmer till tender (about 1½ hours).
- If necessary, thicken the liquid with flour dissolved in a little cold water.
- Put the "stew" into a 9"x5" baking pan. Place a "birdie" in the middle and cover with pastry.
- Bake at 400° F/205° C until pastry is cooked.

Flour Scones

Makes 32 scones

4 cups	Five Roses flour	1 L
2 tbsp	sugar	30 mL
2 tsp	cream of tartar	10 mL
2 tsp	baking soda	10 mL
$\frac{1}{4}$ cup	lard	50 mL
$2\frac{2}{3}$ cups	buttermilk	650 mL

- Put all dry ingredients through the flour sifter, then add the lard.
- Work the batter with your hands until well mixed.
- Add the buttermilk. Work the batter with a knife rather than a fork or a spoon.
- Grandmother prefers the batter to be a little moist, then she can work with the dough coated with flour.
- Turn the batter out onto a floured flat surface. Shape into eight equal rounds. Cut each round into four. Flatten to approximately $\frac{1}{2}$" thick.
- The scones should be roughly triangular.
- Cook in an ungreased electric frying pan at 400° F/205° C until brown.
- Cook the scones on each side and on the ends. Brown all the sides for complete cooking.

Recipe Hints

If Grandmother's cooking is noted for anything it is her flour scones. The original recipe is lost to antiquity, since she learned the methods and the components from her mother, who learned them from her mother, who . . . and it goes on back many generations. Great-grandmother made the scones on a huge iron griddle over a wood-burning stove.

As a pre-teenager and a teenager it was my job on a Sunday morning to ride my bicycle to Great-grandmother Gillespie's house to get the scones for lunch. This was a weekly treat right up to her death.

Then Grandmother took over the task of making the scones at home. The next generation? Who knows?

Working the batter with a table knife is traditional. Great-grandmother did it that way, therefore Grandmother does.

Two-thirds litre of buttermilk is approximate. The batter should be moist but not sloppy.

There is no grease or oil in the fry pan during the cooking.
Many of us like the scones with just butter. Others get fancy
with jam, cheese and almost any condiment associated with a
sandwich.

*Grandmother's goodies were part of every pic-
nic. Left to right: Uncle Eric, Grandmother,
Aunt Evelyn, Lois and Phillip. This photograph was taken at York, on the Grand River,
in the summer of 1943.*

Fruit Loaf

¼ cup	Butter	125 mL
2 cups	sugar	500 mL
2	eggs	
2 tsp	vanilla	10 mL
1½ cups	milk	375 mL
3 tsp	baking powder	15 mL
3 cups	Monarch cake flour	725 mL
1 cup	raisins	250 mL
1 cup	currants	250 mL

- Cream the butter and the sugar. Mix in eggs and vanilla. Add the milk.
- Mix the baking powder and flour.
- Add to the butter mix.
- Add the raisins and currants.
- Pour batter into loaf pans lined with wax paper.
- Bake at 325° F/165° C for 1 hour.

Lemon Loaf

⅓ cup	butter	75 mL
1 cup	sugar	250 mL
2	eggs	
1½ cups	Monarch cake and pastry flour	375 mL
½ cup	walnuts or coconut	125 mL
¼ cup	maraschino cherries	50 mL
½ cup	milk	125 mL
1 tsp	baking powder	5 mL
½ tsp	salt	2 mL
	rind and juice of 1 lemon	

- Cream the butter and the sugar.
- Add the eggs and the remaining ingredients. Do not add the lemon juice at this time.
- Bake in a 9"x5"x3" greased loaf pan.
- Bake at 350° F/180° C for 1 hour.
- Remove from the oven. While hot, glaze with lemon juice and ¼ cup sugar mixture.
- Let stand a few hours before cutting.

Banana Bran Muffins

2 cups	ripe bananas	500 mL
1 cup	buttermilk	250 mL
1/3 cup	molasses	75 mL
2	eggs	
1 tbsp	butter (melted)	15 mL
2 cups	oat bran	500 mL
1/2 cup	Five Roses whole wheat flour	125 mL
1/2 cup	walnuts (chopped fine)	125 mL
1/4 tsp	salt	1 mL
1/2 tsp	nutmeg	2 mL
1/2 tsp	cinnamon	2 mL
1/2 tsp	baking soda	2 mL
1 tsp	baking powder (heaping)	5 mL

Raisins, currants, chopped dates and figs can be added as desired.

- Mix all ingredients.
- Drop batter into a greased muffin tin.
- Bake at 350° F/180° C for 10 minutes.
- The ideal bananas to use are those which have turned almost black but are not bad or rotting. As with the Banana Cake, the bananas can also be frozen until ready to be used. Thaw before using.

Health Muffins

1	egg	
³⁄₄ cup	brown sugar	175 mL
³⁄₄ cup	sour cream	175 mL
¹⁄₂ cup	sunflower oil	125 mL
1 cup	Five Roses flour	250 mL
¹⁄₂ cup	wheat germ	125 mL
1 cup	oat bran	250 mL
¹⁄₄ tsp	salt	1 mL
¹⁄₂ tsp	baking powder	2 mL
1 tsp	baking soda	5 mL
2 cups	dates (chopped)	500 mL

- Cream the sugar with the eggs.
- Add the sour cream and the oil.
- Mix well.
- Add the dry ingredients gradually.
- Drop batter into a greased muffin tin.
- Bake at 350° F/180° C for 20-25 minutes.
- A mixture of wheat and oat brans can be used.

British Yorkshire Pudding

2 cups	Five Roses flour	500 mL
1/4 tsp	salt and pepper	1 mL
2 1/2 cups	milk	625 mL
4	eggs	
1 1/4 cups	water	300 mL

- Preheat oven to 450° F/230° C.
- Mix the flour, salt and pepper together.
- Add the milk, eggs and water to form the batter.
- Allow the batter to stand for an hour. In the oven, heat the drippings from the roast of beef in a muffin tray, approximately 1/4 tsp in each mould.
- Pour in the batter.
- Cook in 450° F/230° C oven until it has risen, then lower the temperature to 350° F/180° C for 40-45 minutes.

Alternately

- Put 1/2 cup of roast dripping in a 13"x9" pan.
- Add the batter. Bake at 420° F/210° C for 30 minutes.

Macaroni and Cheese

1	6-ounce package of 7-minute macaroni	
1	10-ounce can of mushroom soup	
½ cup	milk	125 mL
1 tsp	onion (grated)	5 mL
1½ cup	old cheddar cheese	375 mL
½ tsp	salt	2 mL
	dash of pepper	

- Cook the macaroni in boiling water. Rinse in cold water when cooked.
- Combine the mushroom soup, milk, onions, cheese and seasonings. Add to the macaroni.
- Bake in a 1½ quart baking dish at 350° F/180° C for 45 minutes.

Recipe Hint

The recipe can be prepared well ahead of time and warmed for a quick lunch or snack.

Potato Scones

- The amounts used vary according to the amount of mashed potatoes available.
- The original "recipe" (there is no written recipe) calls for the cook to hand-mix equal quantities of potatoes and flour.
- I find that a hand mixer does a better job of mixing the flour and the potatoes. Mix until you have a mixing bowl containing grain-sized pellets of flour and potatoes. Into this mixture pour a small, warm glass of warm milk. The ensuing mix will be damp and sticky.
- Form snowball-sized balls of the dough by sprinkling the dough liberally with flour, which enables handling. Spread flour over a flat surface. Place a doughball on the flour and roll it flat with a floured rolling pin. Maintain a coat of flour at all times to avoid sticking.
- Roll the dough flat, about the size of the frying pan and ⅛" thick.
- Cut the flattened dough into four triangular pieces.
- Cook the scones in a preheated Teflon frying pan at a high heat. *Do not add oil to the frying pan.* They should be cooked on a dry surface.
- Turn each scone as it begins to brown on each side.
- Line a dinner plate with tea towels.
- Stack the scones on the towels; wrap to retain the moisture and the heat. Keep warm in the oven until ready to serve.
- Serve with butter, cheese or anything else you fancy. Roll the buttered scone into a cylinder and eat it from your hand.
- Note: The potatoes should have salt, buttermilk and pepper added in the process of being mashed.
- New potatoes do not work well in this recipe; old potatoes or baking potatoes are best for the task.

Recipe Hints

This is another griddle recipe. Great-grandmother Gillespie made these "scones" on a large iron griddle over a wood-burning stove.

Grandmother prefers the potatoes to be a little warm when she is making the batter. However, if the potatoes have been stored in the refrigerator and are cool, a small glass of warm milk can be added to them.

These are called potato scones, but in shape and form they more closely resemble a soft Mexican tortilla.

We usually save the leftover mashed potatoes for a week and then make a batch of scones for a meal.

To the ingredients shown, add a liberal amount of good guesses and experience.

The picnics became a little more sedate as the elders got older. Pictured here at Queenston Heights are (left to right) Grandfather Kettle, Uncle Bob Still, Uncle Eric Kettle and Ben Pounder.

Scotch Pancakes

2 cups	Five Roses flour	500 mL
1 tsp	baking soda	5 mL
1 tsp	baking powder	5 mL
1 tbsp	butter (softened)	15 mL
$\frac{1}{2}$ cup	sugar	125 mL
1	egg	
$\frac{1}{2}$ tsp	salt	2 mL

- Rub the butter into the dry ingredients. Add the milk and the egg. Pour batter onto pan.
- Fry in an ungreased Teflon frying pan.

Recipe Hints

These pancakes were used like sweet buns. They were served with butter and jam for afternoon tea.